100 Money Solutions

Simplifying Your Road to Wealth

Kenneth GITA Taylor | **www.100moneysolutions.com**

Copyright © 2018 by Kenneth GITA Taylor

All rights reserved. No part of this publication may be reproduced, distributed, or transmitted in any form or by any means, including photocopying, recording, or other electronic or mechanical methods, without the prior written permission of the publisher, except in the case of brief quotations embodied in critical reviews and certain other noncommercial uses permitted by copyright law.

For permission requests, contact the publisher directly using the contact information below.

Address: I Am Whitney Sherrill, LLC
5245 NW 195th Terr
Miami Gardens, Fl 33055
Email: iamwhitneysherrill@gmail.com
Ph: (305) 563-4484

Ordering Information:
Special discounts are available on quantity purchases by certain groups, organizations, and associations. For orders by U.S. trade bookstores and wholesalers, corporations, and others, contact the publisher using the contact information above.

Original written content by Kenneth GITA Taylor

Edited by Whitney Sherrill, M.A., Ed.D.

Cover graphic & design by Whitney Sherrill, M.A., Ed.D.

Format & arrangement by Kenneth GITA Taylor & Whitney Sherrill, M.A., Ed.D.

Printed in the United States of America

Acknowledgments

Special thanks to the WealthWave Team, and all friends, family, clients, and supporters along the journey to realizing the dream!

Table of Contents

Stage I: Protection

Stage II: Do's & Don'ts

Stage III: Growth

Stage IV: Preservation

Stage I

Protection

Money Solution #1

Check your account balances and recent transactions daily.

Kenneth GITA Taylor | www.100moneysolutions.com

Money Solution #2

Review your retirement statements (fees and returns) annually.

Money Solution #3

Pay your bills on time and manage your checking account wisely in order to avoid unnecessary fees.

Money Solution #4

Make your primary financial institution your homepage to ensure that you stay on top of it all.

Kenneth GITA Taylor | www.100moneysolutions.com

Money Solution #5

Credit is power, so protect yours.

Among other things, your credit score will determine your **interest rate** if you decide to apply for a loan or line of credit.

Money Solution #6

Refrain from accumulating credit card debt or using credit without a clearly defined and justifiable purpose.

Kenneth GITA Taylor | www.100moneysolutions.com

Money Solution #7

Review your credit report annually, and take the time to dispute any inaccurate or outdated information.

Money Solution #8

Download a reputable app to regularly monitor and review your credit accounts.

Kenneth GITA Taylor | www.100moneysolutions.com

Money Solution #9

You have
insurance on
your car
and your home...

Why not *yourself?*

Kenneth GITA Taylor | www.100moneysolutions.com

Money Solution #10

Consider changing your health insurance plan from a PPO to an HMO or EPO.

HMO (health maintenance organization)

EPO (exclusive provider organization)

PPO (preferred provider organization)

Kenneth GITA Taylor | www.100moneysolutions.com

Money Solution #11

Be sure to get a policy that provides long-term care and disability coverage.

*7 out of 10 people will have a **long-term care event.***

Money Solution #12

Have a plan to deal with identity theft.

It's often not a matter of *if,* but *when* it will happen.

Kenneth GITA Taylor | www.100moneysolutions.com

Money Solution #13

Protect yourself from scam artists!

It has unfortunately become a common practice to prey on others and manipulate peoples' vulnerabilities.

Money Solution #14

Don't make the same money mistake over and over.

Kenneth GITA Taylor | www.100moneysolutions.com

Money Solution #15

Never compromise your values just to make money.

Kenneth GITA Taylor | www.100moneysolutions.com

Money Solution #16

Be discerning and question unrealistic returns.

Kenneth GITA Taylor | www.100moneysolutions.com

Money Solution #17

Always do your due diligence before making an investment.

Kenneth GITA Taylor | www.100moneysolutions.com

Money Solution #18

If it seems
too good
to be true…

it probably is.

Kenneth GITA Taylor | **www.100moneysolutions.com**

Money Solution #19

Diversification is the key to minimizing risk.

Don't put all your eggs in one basket.

Money Solution #20

You can save a ton of money by buying groceries and eating more home-cooked or self-prepared meals.

Strive to eat out only occasionally.

Money Solution #21

Don't waste too much of your money on depreciating items.

If you keep buying things you do not need, soon you will have to sell things you need.

~Warren Buffett

Money Solution #22

Avoid buying a big, beautiful home that leaves you "cash-poor."

Don't end up with an *awesome* house and *no* money.

Kenneth GITA Taylor | www.100moneysolutions.com

Money Solution #23

Before making any large purchases, sleep on it for a night.

Decide what constitutes a large purchase (ex: $250+)

Kenneth GITA Taylor | www.100moneysolutions.com

Money Solution #24

If you decide to lend money, be sure to have the borrower sign a promissory letter.

Yes, this applies to friends and family, too.

Money Solution #25

You are constantly becoming an average of the five people you hang around most.

Your company can and will transform you (for better or for worse), so choose your associations wisely.

Kenneth GITA Taylor | www.100moneysolutions.com

Stage II

Do's

& Don'ts

Money Solution #26

Write down your financial goals regularly.

Kenneth GITA Taylor | www.100moneysolutions.com

Money Solution #27

Budgets help you to track your income and expenses and more clearly identify your financial goals.

Money Solution #28

Create a 12-week year and renew your financial goals every 12 weeks.

Kenneth GITA Taylor | **www.100moneysolutions.com**

Money Solution #29

Set some clear financial deadlines for yourself and make every effort to meet them.

Kenneth GITA Taylor | www.100moneysolutions.com

Money Solution #30

Treat your money like a valued companion...

*The more attention you pay
to your money,
the longer it will stay with you.*

Money Solution #31

Time *is* money…

Don't waste *either*.

Money Solution #32

Slow and steady wins the race...

AVOID get-rich-quick schemes!

Kenneth GITA Taylor | www.100moneysolutions.com

Money Solution #33

Don't feel rushed or pressured into home-buying; take your time to find the right neighborhood.

Money Solution #34

Create savings games and incentive/reward systems to further motivate and encourage you to reach your savings goals.

Money Solution #35

Stash away the equivalent of *at least* 3 months of your total expenses in a liquid emergency fund.

Kenneth GITA Taylor | www.100moneysolutions.com

Money Solution #36

When selecting a credit card, choose one that offers 0% APR, no annual fee, and rewards, like points or cash-back.

Kenneth GITA Taylor | www.100moneysolutions.com

Money Solution #37

Cars depreciate, and expensive car payments ravenously consume your income; avoid them at all costs!

Money Solution #38

Extended warranties are money-suckers; it is best to avoid them.

Money Solution #39

Pay down your debts in order of smallest to largest.

This approach will allow you to pay off individual debtors faster and observe measurable progress.

Kenneth GITA Taylor | www.100moneysolutions.com

Money Solution #40

If you have a credit and/or debt problem, please seek professional assistance.

Money Solution #41

If you are in student loan debt, research student loan forgiveness programs.

Money Solution #42

Stay away from payday advance loans!

Kenneth GITA Taylor | www.100moneysolutions.com

Money Solution #43

Check to see if your health insurance provider offers a tele-medicine option.

This feature allows you to consult with a medical professional without a mandatory office visit.

Kenneth GITA Taylor | www.100moneysolutions.com

Money Solution #44

Set up a Health Savings Account (HSA) and save money on health expenses.

Kenneth GITA Taylor | www.100moneysolutions.com

Money Solution #45

Review your insurance policies every two years to determine whether additional savings are available to you.

Kenneth GITA Taylor | www.100moneysolutions.com

Money Solution #46

Personal finance is about your behaviors and choices, not necessarily your level of education.

Simply commit to the process of growing your wealth, and avoid feeling intimidated.

Kenneth GITA Taylor | www.100moneysolutions.com

Money Solution #47

Don't work simply to earn money; prioritize your passions.

Kenneth GITA Taylor | www.100moneysolutions.com

Money Solution #48

Aim to achieve a healthy work-life balance.

Money Solution #49

It's not about how much money you make;
it's about how much you keep...

Be sure to spend less than what you make.

Kenneth GITA Taylor | www.100moneysolutions.com

Money Solution #50

The secret is out... the "Jones" are broke.

Don't believe the hype, and never compare yourself to others.

Kenneth GITA Taylor | www.100moneysolutions.com

Stage III

Growth

Money Solution #51

Increasing your financial literacy is the greatest stimulant for wealth-building.

Kenneth GITA Taylor | www.100moneysolutions.com

Money Solution #52

Give your money purpose by allocating it thoughtfully so that it can help you to accomplish your goals.

Kenneth GITA Taylor | www.100moneysolutions.com

Money Solution #53

Downsize rather than supersize your purchases.

Kenneth GITA Taylor | www.100moneysolutions.com

Money Solution #54

Set up an automatic savings feature that easily deducts a set amount from your paycheck and places the funds into an interest-bearing savings account.

Money Solution #55

One man's trash is another man's treasure...

Consider selling some stuff to earn extra money.

Money Solution #56

In every instance, make your money work for *you*.

*Investing in **assets** will help you to generate more income, thereby increasing cash flow.*

Kenneth GITA Taylor | www.100moneysolutions.com

Money Solution #57

Download apps that allow you to save money while spending.

(Ex: *Acorn* and *Stash*)

Money Solution #58

If you shop online, get paid to shop.

*Earn **cash back** by doing your shopping via online portals that offer rewards (ex: Ebates, Ibotta)*

Money Solution #59

Compound interest is the eighth wonder of the world... use it, or it will use you.

Your benefit: *Investment vehicle yielding a high rate of return.*

Your detriment: *Getting in debt and paying a high rate of return.*

Kenneth GITA Taylor | www.100moneysolutions.com

Money Solution #60

If you open an Individual Retirement Account (IRA), opt for a Roth IRA in order to take advantage of tax-free gains.

Retirees <50 years of age can make a max contribution of *$5500/year.*

Retirees 50+ years of age can make a max contribution of *$6500/year.*

Kenneth GITA Taylor | www.100moneysolutions.com

Money Solution #61

If you opt not to hire a professional money manager, consider an index fund as a safe and inexpensive investment option.

Money Solution #62

Real estate is a great investment strategy to earn large lump sums of money with tax benefits.

Kenneth GITA Taylor | www.100moneysolutions.com

Money Solution #63

There are multiple strategies in real estate investing; you have to find the right strategy for you, your goals, your skill sets, and your market.

Strategies include wholesale, fix and flip, commercial, single family rentals, foreclosures, tax liens, promissory note or commercial paper, buy and hold, and passive investments.

Kenneth GITA Taylor | www.100moneysolutions.com

Money Solution #64

When it comes to your 401(k), only contribute an amount equal to the percentage that your employer is matching.

*If your employer offers it, request a **Roth 401(k)** to take advantage of tax-free gains.*

Kenneth GITA Taylor | www.100moneysolutions.com

Money Solution #65

Selling your primary residence after two years qualifies you for exemption from the associated capital gain tax.

Kenneth GITA Taylor | www.100moneysolutions.com

Money Solution #66

The financial services industry is constantly changing, so be sure to stay abreast of new products, benefits, and in-roads to wealth.

Kenneth GITA Taylor | www.100moneysolutions.com

Money Solution #67

Increase your earning potential through personal and professional development.

The best investment that you can make is in *yourself*.

Kenneth GITA Taylor | www.100moneysolutions.com

Money Solution #68

It's never too late to learn a new, lucrative skill.

Kenneth GITA Taylor | www.100moneysolutions.com

Money Solution #69

Don't get a second job... start a side business!

Work to develop
multiple streams of income.

Money Solution #70

It's far better to buy a great company at a fair price than a fair company at a great price.

Kenneth GITA Taylor | www.100moneysolutions.com

Money Solution #71

Consider free-lancing as a means to earn extra income; it can be very lucrative.

Kenneth GITA Taylor | www.100moneysolutions.com

Money Solution #72

Brand yourself.

*Establishing yourself as brand increases your **value** in the market, allowing you to request higher compensation for all that you do.*

Money Solution #73

Create something that adds a tremendous amount of value to the world.

Innovation gives rise to wealth.

Kenneth GITA Taylor | www.100moneysolutions.com

Money Solution #74

Being rich and powerful comes at a price... are you willing to pay it?

Kenneth GITA Taylor | www.100moneysolutions.com

Money Solution #75

Wealth-building requires time, so be patient with yourself.

Kenneth GITA Taylor | www.100moneysolutions.com

Stage IV

Preservation

Money Solution #76

Investing is a long-term rather than short-term endeavor.

Remember that your financial future is *ever-approaching*.

Kenneth GITA Taylor | www.100moneysolutions.com

Money Solution #77

Always move at least 10% of your income into your personal savings account before paying any bills.

It's the **"pay yourself first"** principle.

Kenneth GITA Taylor | www.100moneysolutions.com

Money Solution #78

Always move at least 10% of your income into an active investment account.

Another way to keep your money working for you.

Kenneth GITA Taylor | www.100moneysolutions.com

Money Solution #79

It is a great practice to allocate 10% of your income to tithes or charity.

Kenneth GITA Taylor | www.100moneysolutions.com

Money Solution #80

If you strive to live off of no more than 70% of your income, you can avoid unnecessary financial stressors.

Kenneth GITA Taylor | www.100moneysolutions.com

Money Solution #81

Get a professional to help manage your money.

Statistics show that people with money managers typically retire with more money than those without money managers.

Money Solution #82

Make sure that your financial professional has fiduciary responsibility.

An advisor with **Suitability Standards** is primarily concerned with the affordability of the product.

An advisor with **Fiduciary Responsibility** is required by law to act in the best interest of the client regardless of whether there is financial benefit for himself/herself.

Kenneth GITA Taylor | www.100moneysolutions.com

Money Solution #83

To become wealthy, invest *early* and *often*!

Kenneth GITA Taylor | www.100moneysolutions.com

Money Solution #84

Start investing for your children *as early as possible,* no matter the amount.

Kenneth GITA Taylor | www.100moneysolutions.com

Money Solution #85

Create a plan to cut off your adult children whose expenses can eat into your earned wealth.

Money Solution #86

Estate planning is not just for the elderly or ailing; it's for *everyone*.

Start working on it as soon as possible.

Kenneth GITA Taylor | www.100moneysolutions.com

Money Solution #87

Be sure to establish a beneficiary on all of your accounts.

Kenneth GITA Taylor | www.100moneysolutions.com

Money Solution #88

Set up your retirement account as soon as possible in order to secure a more financially prosperous and comfortable retirement.

Kenneth GITA Taylor | www.100moneysolutions.com

Money Solution #89

Explore as many tax-free strategies as possible.

Money Solution #90

Spend the interest of your investment, never the principle.

Let the principle continue to work for you!

Kenneth GITA Taylor | www.100moneysolutions.com

Money Solution #91

Build a portfolio of investments, acquire assets, and limit liabilities.

Kenneth GITA Taylor | www.100moneysolutions.com

Money Solution #92

Review your expense ratio for any and all investment instruments.

$$\frac{fund\ operating\ expense}{value\ of\ fund} = expense\ ratio$$

Money Solution #93

Pigs get fed; hogs get slaughtered.

Avoid excessive greed.

Money Solution #94

When negotiating, listen more than you speak.

This practice helps you to make better, more informed decisions.

Kenneth GITA Taylor | www.100moneysolutions.com

Money Solution #95

Create a financial plan and track your net worth monthly.

$$\frac{\begin{array}{r}(Assets)\\ - \ (Liabilities)\end{array}}{= \textbf{\textit{Net Worth}}}$$

Money Solution #96

Over-estimate your financial needs.

When it comes to retirement, most people underestimate how much they will need; if not mindful, one can run the risk of outliving his/her available funds.

Money Solution #97

Discuss, clarify, and agree upon finance-related goals with your spouse.

Kenneth GITA Taylor | www.100moneysolutions.com

Money Solution #98

Faith, family, friends, finance, fitness and fun are cornerstones of your overall success.

Kenneth GITA Taylor | www.100moneysolutions.com

Money Solution #99

Your health and your wealth are positively correlated...

*Make your **personal care** a priority.*

Money Solution #100

Never stop dreaming.

Your dreams will fuel your wealth-building endeavors and **fortify your "why."**

About the Author

Like many Americans, Kenneth GITA Taylor came from humble beginnings. Although times weren't always easy, he remained determined to strive for more. He excelled through school and successfully completed a Bachelor of Science from the University of South Florida with majors in Business Management and Hospitality Management. While pursuing his undergraduate degree, he worked full time for a reputable and well-known banking institution, and throughout that time, he developed a passion for finance and for helping others navigate the roads to financial freedom.

He has spent the last 15 years in the financial industry developing a robust expertise in the world of personal finance, credit, lending, and investment. As a credentialed, fully-licensed, and seasoned Investment Advisor Representative, his financial knowledge base and business acumen is unparalleled. Each and every day he works to further his mission of helping one million people become millionaires; it was from this mission that *100 Money Solutions* was birthed.

www.ingramcontent.com/pod-product-compliance
Lightning Source LLC
Chambersburg PA
CBHW020443220526
45464CB00002B/836